Introduction: Dreams Don't Wait

When I was 14, I didn't really know what I was doing with my life. Although I knew that I was not planning to wait for life to hand me opportunities, just sit back, and just let things happen for me. Most people my age were focused on school and sports, and yes, I was too. But this was something I couldn't ignore; it was a feeling that I wanted more than just the usual path. I wanted to create something of my own. I wanted to be different, so I believed that I would regret it if I didn't start my journey now. And that's how my journey began.

Now that I look back, it is kind of crazy to think that I was able to turn some fun into a full working business, earning six figures before I even turned 16. Instead of thinking, 'How can I, just 15 years old, think about something so big?', I pushed myself forward and formed a talented team.

The journey started very small; I didn't wake up one day and have a full working business; it began with multiple meetings, research, and trying something new. I was able to connect with a successful young entrepreneur who shared the same vision as me, Sebastian. He was the CEO of a real estate company that he started at 16 years old. Together, we built "Korseo Capital Exchange," a gold exchange company with a team of nine dedicated people who believed in what we were doing.

At first, it was overwhelming; managing time between school, friends, and family wasn't very easy. There were many days when I felt like I was just wasting my time. But I realized that the best way to learn is by doing it. We made a lot of mistakes at the start, but it taught us more valuable lessons. We learned how to communicate better, how to adapt to challenges, and to never quit even when things get difficult.

I didn't have years of experience, but I had determination, a supportive team, and the willingness to step outside my comfort zone. Looking back at it, one of the most important lessons I've learned is that age does not define capability. No one is ever truly ready; you become ready by starting and by taking the first step.

This book is not about showing my success or that I have all the knowledge; it is about showing that it's possible to dream big, no matter where you are starting from. This book is for anyone who's ever had an idea but didn't know where to start; it is for curious minds, dreamers, and risk-takers who know that there is more to life than following the usual path.

Your dreams should never wait; the best time to start is never gone. It is now. I hope that this book will inspire you to take your first step. Together, we will explore the world of entrepreneurship and the power of persistence. It is worth it.

Now that I look back, it is kind of crazy to think that I was able to turn some fun into a full working business, earning six figures before I even turned 16. Instead of thinking 'How can I at just 15 years old think about something so big?', I pushed myself forward and formed a talented team.

The journey started very small, I didn't wake up one day and had a full working business, it began with multiple meetings, research and trying something new. I was able to connect with a successful young entrepreneur who shared the same vision as me, Sebastian. He was the CEO of a real estate company which he started at 16 years old. Together, we built "Korseo Capital

Exchange", a gold exchange company with a team of nine dedicated people who believed in what we were doing.

At first, it was overwhelming, managing time between school, friends and family wasn't very easy, there were many days when I felt like I was just wasting my time. But I realized that the best way to learn is by doing it. We made a lot of mistakes at the start but it taught us more valuable lessons. We learned how to communicate better, how to adapt to challenges and to never quit even when things get difficult.

I didn't have years of experience but I had determination, a supportive team and the willingness to step outside my comfort zone. Looking back at it, one of the most important lessons I've learned is that age does not define capability. No one is ever truly ready, you become ready by starting and by taking the first step.

This book is not about showing my success or that I have all the knowledge, it is about showing that it's possible to dream big, no matter where you are starting from. This book is for anyone who's ever had an idea but didn't know where to start, it is for curious minds, dreamers and risk takers who know that there is more to life than following the usual path.

Your dreams should never wait, the best time to start is never gone. It is now. I hope that this book will inspire you to take your first step. Together, we will explore the world of entrepreneurship and the power of persistence. It is worth it.

Chapter 1: A Teenager's Mindset: The Key to Success

So, what does a right mindset mean? It's not about working non-stop or convincing yourself that success is just about grinding harder than everyone else. A right mindset is about seeing opportunities where others see obstacles, it's about believing in your ability to learn, adapt and improve.

At this age, we are told to focus on school and we continue to wait for the "right time" to start chasing our dreams, but there is no perfect time to start. I was not a genius but I had curiosity about how businesses worked and how someone like me without much experience could get into this field. Mindset is all about how you view the world and see the challenges, setbacks and opportunities around you.

THE STORY OF FAILURE
Everyone has the fear of failure, 'What if this does not work out and people judge me?' When I partnered with Sebastian, we didn't have a deep understanding of the market and were trying to figure everything out. I remember the first time we pitched a client and completely ruined the

agreement. We didn't have clear answers and felt like we were hopeless. But instead of letting that experience discourage us, we thought of it as a way to improve. Every time something doesn't go as planned, we need to learn and improve from it. *"Failure isn't the opposite of success; it's part of the journey to success."*

SELF DOUBT - *a silent enemy*

Let's talk about self doubt, there is a voice in our head which says, "You can't do it, you're too young or not experienced". I questioned whether anyone would take me seriously in the business world. I wondered if I had what it took to make ideas turn to reality. Everyone experiences self doubt but the key is not letting it stop you.

I used to focus on small achievable goals instead of trying to solve everything at once. When we first decided to start with this work, we did not start looking for clients. We had to register our business, get all the business licenses that are required, decide on the kinds of gold we are going to buy and sell, learn about the gold valuation and so much more. Earning doesn't start immediately, it requires proper planning and preparation. Surrounding yourself with people who believe in you is one of the best ways to silence self doubt.

CHOOSING THE RIGHT PEOPLE

Success is not a one person's work, behind every great business is a team of people working together towards a dream. When I look back at my journey, I realize how important it is to have the right people with me. Partnering with Sebastian was one of the best decisions I had made. We were totally different in skills but shared the same vision, he was good at organizing, planning and making sure everything worked smoothly, we balanced each other out and that is what made our team strong.

But finding the right people isn't about skills, it's more about having the same goals and trust is the most important element. If you don't trust the people you are working with, it would be difficult to move on. Have someone you can rely on during tough times. Another thing I learned is that people around you should challenge and inspire you, it is not always helpful to have a team which agrees with everything you say, you should always provide suggestions, make your plans better.

What really matters is how you handle the disagreements, we made sure to focus on the bigger picture, our vision of building a successful business. Building the right network outside your team is also important, we didn't have all the answers, I reached out to experienced people like him for advice and guidance which helped us to avoid mistakes and understand things we didn't know before.

In the end, having the right people with you makes all the difference, when your team shares the goals and work with you, even the most difficult things become easy, with the right people, the journey to success is more meaningful.

POWER OF PREPARATION

When we were starting a business, excitement can make you want to jump in and just start earning at the start, but I learned that preparation is the key to success, at the start we were not finding customers, we focused on building a strong foundation for the company and started to understand the industry we were entering.

Our first step was research, we spent weeks learning about the valuation, market trends and found out what the buyers and sellers care about the most and require. Knowing how the industry works give you more confidence to make better decisions.,

Another important part of the preparation was handling the legal and technical requirements. Starting a business is not only about a good idea, we need to make sure that we are following all the rules and are legal. We had registered our business, got licenses and understood the legal aspects of trading gold. These steps took a lot of time but they helped us avoid any issues in the future which is proper planning.

Preparation also means planning for challenges, business is unpredictable and things don't always go as we think, we knew there could be delays or changes in the market. One of the most important things we did was break our work into smaller steps and divide it amongst the team. We focused on completing one task at a time, first we registered our business, then we got our license, after that we focused on learning how to value gold properly which made our process much simpler.

Preparation is not only about knowing what to do, it is about building the confidence to face challenges. When you have done the work to understand your business, you feel like you are ready to face any challenges. Looking back, I realized that preparation saved us from making many mistakes, it gave us the opportunity to make things work perfectly because the time we took to plan, we were ready to face any challenges on the way.

CURIOSITY

Curiosity might be one of the most important parts in such fields as it motivates us to ask questions, explore ideas and continue to keep learning. When we started this business, curiosity helped us stay adaptable as the business world keeps changing, we were able to identify new opportunities and keep growing. As the more you learn, the more fun and easy your journey gets

OPTIMISM

When things get tough, it is normal to feel discouraged. There were times when we felt like we couldn't succeed in this, many deals were canceled, we were missing deadlines and had high tension. Optimism doesn't mean ignoring your problems or just pretending it's going to be fine. It's about focusing on solutions instead of worrying, it isn't about being naive, it's about choosing to see possibilities and believing in yourself, your team and your vision even when the journey is tough.

STAYING GROUNDED

Success, no matter how big or small can be exciting, it is easy to get distracted on celebrating and thinking that you have figured everything out. But the time you stop learning more is the moment you stop growing. One of the best pieces of advice I have ever received is "Always be a student". Even as your business continued to grow and we started seeing results, I learned more from competitors and kept looking for ways to improve. Staying grounded is not about being humble, it is about longevity, the more we learn, the more we evolve.

TAKEAWAYS FOR BUILDING A STRONG MINDSET

Embracing failure, you should always see it as a stepping stone and not something which is blocking your path. Focus on small wins and surround yourself with positive people. Stay curious, keep learning, asking questions and exploring new ideas, believe in your ability to overcome challenges.

SEEING OPPORTUNITIES

One of the most powerful aspects of a right mindset is to use all the opportunities you get, the way you face challenges can make all the difference in your journey towards success, the shift in perspective is what helps entrepreneurs move forward.

When we started our business, we faced a lot of challenges, the first pitch we made to a potential client didn't go as planned as we had no properly formed answers to their questions, instead of letting that failure stop us we chose to look at it as an opportunity to improve.

Failure is always an opportunity in disguise, instead of seeing it as something that negaitive, understand it as a lesson, the mistakes we make at the start teach us the importance. We realized that we needed to improve a lot to understand our client's need.

We kept looking for new opportunities to grow our business, we explored new markets, tried different strategies and kept challenging ourselves, in every failure, there was an opportunity to improve. Another valuable lesson I've learned is that opportunity doesn't always come in a clear way, it might be a mistake, challenge or something that is blocking you but might help you in the future. Instead of quitting, try to keep going and know that every challenge you face is just another step towards your dreams.

Building the right mindset is a journey in itself which takes time and effort. Everyday is an opportunity to strengthen your mindset and move closer to achieving your dreams. You should always stay focused and continue to learn and achieve more.

Chapter 2: Turning Ideas into Reality

Starting a business sounds is definately an exciting journey, the first step feels like the hardest. When I first decided to learn everything about the business world , I didn't have much experienec, but I had a strong desire to learn. The key to starting your journey is taking the first step.

At the start, it feels like the learning is never ending, it might seem like you need to know everything before even starting. But no one starts off with all knowledge; entrepreneurship is about figuring things out as you move forward, and the most important part is just to get started. I wanted to understand how businesses operated, how a business succeeds, how we find clients, and how we turn ideas into products or services. I didn't have all the resources or a detailed plan, but I had determination. I took time to research the industry, talked with experienced people, and started small.

THE IMPORTANCE OF STARTING SMALL

A mistake that many new entrepreneurs make is feeling like they have to build something big at the start but the best way to learn and grow is by starting small. When you start your journey with small and manageable goals, it makes the whole process much more enjoyable and easier.

I started my business by focusing on the basics step by step: As I completed each small task, I could feel the progress and confidence to handle bigger challenges.

Starting small helps us to test our ideas and improve them as we try; it is an opportunity to learn what works and what doesn't before committing too much time or resources. For example, when I was learning about the gold market, I began with researching, testing, and learning how the market can fluctuate with smaller transactions.

OVERCOMING THE FEAR

There is always a fear or nervousness of not knowing enough or being unprepared. The key is not letting that fear stop you. No one is ever fully prepared for anything, but that should not stop you from trying. Even though I didn't have all the knowledge at the start, I began to learn, adapt, and improve. In this chapter, we will explore how to turn your curiosity and motivation into reality and how to build your foundation and face challenges with confidence.

TURNING IDEAS TO REALITY

Turning your business ideas into reality is one of the challenging parts of entrepreneurship, it might be easy to come up with great ideas, but turning them into reality requires a lot of effort, persistence, and dedication.

In the beginning, you might have a vision or an idea; you see the possibilities but wonder how to make it all happen.

CLARIFYING YOUR IDEA

The first step is to turn the idea into reality to clarify it. Ask yourself some questions: What exactly is your idea? What problem does it solve, and who is it for?. Without such clear answers, your idea will remain just an idea. The more specific you learn about your product or service, the easier your journey becomes.

When I started out, I had an idea of what I wanted to do but wasn't completely sure about the process or details. If it was going to be a big business? The more I researched and formed my ideas, the more focused I became.

PLANNING YOUR PATH

Once you gain a clear understanding of your idea, you have to make a plan. A business plan that outlines the main steps you need to take to turn your idea into reality. It should cover every single detail, like your product or service, how you plan to reach your audience, and how you would earn. When I began planning, I didn't just think about the final outcome; I thought about the process: how I would develop the product, how I would find customers, how much money I would need to get started, and how long it would take. Without these points, I have no direction, and the idea would have just remained as a dream.

OVERCOMING OBSTACLES

There will always be obstacles when trying to turn ideas into reality, whether it is financial limitation, lack of experience, or unexpected challenges. I faced many challenges such as time constraints, research problems, and self-doubt. But the key to overcoming these obstacles was to stay persistent and find creative solutions. When we didn't have much capital for some products, we tried getting early customers who believed in our vision and got them to invest in us. Every obstacle is an opportunity to learn and grow.

LEARNING AND ADAPTING

The process of turning an idea into reality isn't easy; as you start to execute your plans, you will learn new things about your business, your customers, and yourself. When I first launched my business, I had to learn everything from dealing with suppliers to managing customers; some of the things I thought I knew didn't work out the way I expected, and I had to learn to adapt. Businesses rarely go according to the plan, but we need to be the ones who can adjust their strategy and always keep moving forward.

TESTING AND FEEDBACK

Another important step in turning our ideas into reality is testing your products and services and taking feedback from customers and others, which will help you to improve and ensure you are providing what the customers actually want. Testing doesn't have to be a formal process; it can be as simple as asking for opinions, conducting surveys, or directly observing how the customer reacts to something.

SCALING AND GROWING

Once you test your product/service and make good improvements, it's time to scale. Scaling is expanding your business, reaching more customers, and increasing the quality and quantity. Scaling also has a lot of challenges; it requires marketing and partnerships, but with careful planning and commitment, it is possible to grow your idea into a great business.

BUILDING A STRONG FOUNDATION

A strong foundation is crucial for the success of any business; think of your business as a house: without a strong foundation, the rest of the structure will easily fall. The foundation includes legal structure, financial planning, branding, and the team behind everything.

CHOOSING THE RIGHT BUSINESS STRUCTURE

The first step in building a strong foundation is to choose the right legal structure; this decision will impact everything from your personal liabilities to taxes and how you can raise money. The most common types of business structures include sole proprietorship, partnership, limited liability company, and corporation.

When I started, I spent time understanding the pros and cons of each of these structures. We decided to proceed with LLC because it offers liability protection for personal assets while providing flexibility in how the business is managed and taxed. It is essential to research and choose a structure that fits our goals and offers the protections and benefits that we want.

FINANCIAL PLANNING AND BUDGETING

Having a financial plan in place is another important step in building a proper foundation; it includes budgeting, understanding startup costs, and planning for future expenses. Without a proper financial plan and budget, it can be easy to run out of money before your business becomes profitable. I created a detailed budget that included everything from marketing costs to utilities costs. Keeping track of all these costs helped me to avoid financial stress. We should always plan for unexpected expenses and create a way to help ourselves with any challenges that might come.

CREATING A BRAND IDENTITY

Your brand identity is not just a logo or colors; it is the story you tell about your business, what values you stand for, and how the customers see you. It should define your mission, the tone, and make your business memorable and help build loyalty.

SETTING UP SYSTEMS AND PROCESSES

Systems and processes are what keep your business running smoothly; it includes accounting, inventory management, customer experience, and marketing. You can save a lot of time and reduce errors if you set up clear processes early. I used simple tools like spreadsheets for accounts to track expenses and manage sales. Such online tools can be used for managing emails and automating sales processes. Having well-defined processes is the key to maintaining efficiency and also ensuring consistency.

LEGAL CONSIDERATIONS AND COMPLIANCE

Legal considerations are another important part of building a strong company. We require licenses to register our business, and ensuring that our contracts are solid is very important; legal protection is a very serious and important part to avoid problems in the future. In the beginning, I worked with a lawyer to make sure all our contracts were in order and that we had the right licenses to operate. While legal advice can be expensive, it is an investment that will save me from costly mistakes in the future.

LEARNING FROM MISTAKES: THE EARLY STRUGGLES

Starting a business is not always smooth; mistakes are part of the process, especially in the start. Mistakes and experience teach us valuable lessons that no book or course can. When I reflect on myself, I can see those moments when I was struggling; it made me think about my strategies, improve my skills, and understand what it really takes to build something like this. One of the first challenges we faced was underestimating the importance of details; we were overlooking small aspects like clear pricing and proper communication. It did create a lot of confusion and delay with clients, which taught us to approach every task with proper knowledge, knowing that even a tiny mistake can cause a big effect.
We all assume we can figure it out as we move along, but it leads to missing deadlines and no coordination. Mistakes like these highlight an important truth, which is that no matter how eager you are to start, preparation is something that is not optional; taking time at the start to prepare pays off in the future.

THE ROLE OF REFLECTION

Mistakes are only useful if we take the time to reflect on them. After every project or task, ask yourself 3 questions: What went well? What didn't? What changes could we make next time?. Keeping such a habit of regular reflection is the best way for improvement.

DEFINING THE PURPOSE

One of the first steps we took was finding out the purpose of our business. Why are we doing this? Who are we helping? What makes us different? Answering these questions helped us to have a clear direction. Instead of trying to cater to everyone, we focused on a specific target audience. For example, when we entered this market, we narrowed our focus to individuals looking for reliable and transparent valuation services, which helped us to build trust and specialize in meeting their needs.

STRUCTURING THE BUSINESS

A solid foundation isn't just about ideas; it's about being practical. At the beginning, we might make mistakes of operating without clear roles and responsibilities. Tasks may overlap, and the important details can be missed. But to fix this we should start with providing specific responsibilities based on strengths and weaknesses to each person. We should have documented processes, like how we evaluated gold and how we interact with clients. Use different task management tools and calendars to track progress and meet deadlines.

FINANCIAL DISCIPLINE

A major part of building a foundation is to manage our finances. At the start, we were tempted to spend on flashy marketing or some unnecessary tools. However, as we moved ahead, we realized that we needed to be more careful with budgeting. We implemented a simple rule, which was to only spend money on things that directly added value to the business or improved client satisfaction.

RESEARCH AND KNOWLEDGE

Before directly trying to dive into the field, take the time to understand the market. Research is the cornerstone to build the foundation, as for us, we started to study our competitors, legal requirements, and customer behavior. We learned early on about the importance of transparency in valuation. Clients are more likely to trust businesses that explained every step of the process.

ESTABLISHING TRUST

A proper foundation isn't just about internal processes; it's also about creating a reputation for yourself. For us, trust was everything in this industry where scams are a common thing. To establish trust, we provided detailed invoices for each transaction, allowed clients to observe the valuation process, and clearly communicated about the details and prices.

FACING CHALLENGES HEAD ON

No successful journey is without any obstacles; challenges are a part of starting and growing a business. They also are an opportunity for growth and innovation. One of the first challenges we faced was understanding the market, underestimating the competitors, and also how unpredictable the valuation is. Another challenge was time management, balancing school and personal commitments. These were the times when we felt like there weren't enough hours in the day to do all the tasks.

We obtained certifications in gold valuation to build credibility, which helped us to gain our clients trust and also give us a deeper understanding of our craft.

Time management challenges forced us to be more disciplined as we started to schedule our days more effectively, set clear priorities, and start using productivity tools to stay on track. Like many young entrepreneurs, we didn't have unlimited funds to work with; budgeting was one of the toughest challenges we faced. When we needed marketing, we tried free platforms like social media to promote the business, which saved money and also taught us how to be resourceful.

Another challenge is to deal with difficult clients; not every interaction goes smoothly; some clients doubt our work, question our prices, or just have high expectations. Instead of letting these situations set us back, we used to modify our customer approach. Starting to listen patiently, providing clear explanations, and showing empathy, which turns the challenging clients into loyal clients.

Challenges may feel frustrating, but they are essential to growth. It helps us build resilience and sharpen problem-solving skills. Without facing all the challenges, our business wouldn't be where it is today. Challenges are not your enemies; they are actually opportunities in disguise. By facing difficult challenges with a positive mindset, we can overcome, become stronger, and improve.

LEARNING NEW SKILLS

Adapting requires stepping out of your comfort zone and learning new things. For me, I had to improve public speaking, speak confidently to clients, and practice speaking clear English. Also to learn how to negotiate effectively, which would help us secure better deals and partnerships.

THE POWER OF NETWORKING AND CONNECTING WITH THE RIGHT PEOPLE

In business, it's not only about what you know; it's more about who you know. Networking is one of the most powerful tools for any entrepreneur, especially when starting your journey. Connecting with the right people is like easily opening doors to success; you can gain opportunities, guidance, and help your business grow.

When I started, I took advice from a few experienced professionals I knew; these mentors provided me with such knowledge I wouldn't have been able to gain on my own. I learned the importance of creating a reputation, especially in such a field where trust is an important element. If you don't know where to start, reach out to people who inspire you. Attend seminars, join groups, or send an email, and you might get a reply. Most people are willing to share their experience or knowledge if you have respect for them.

Networking isn't just about learning from those ahead of you; it helps you to understand the challenges you are going to face, get support, resources, or maybe even partner up. It isn't just a time activity; it's an ongoing process. Relationships take time to develop and give an impact on the long term; the connections we have since day 1 are still valuable today, even if they are helping with suggestions, advice, or any kind of work.

STAYING FOCUSED, MANAGING DISTRACTIONS, AND OVERCOMING DOUBTS

In the world of entrepreneurship, staying focused is one of the hardest but most important skills we need to develop; there are many distractions, self-doubt, and the constant pressure to succeed. At the start of our business, one of the biggest challenges was this: we were jumping between multiple tasks, learning new things, and had many pros and cons. I found myself spending too much time on social media; the key to staying focused is to find out what is distracting you and set clear boundaries. It can be limiting screen time, focusing on specific tasks at a time, and sometimes sacrificing things to help yourself for the better.

When everything feels urgent, it can be difficult to decide; I realized that prioritizing tasks based on their impact is more important; for example, building better relationships with clients is more important than trying to perfect an exact color for the logo. It is more important to focus on creating proper services, building a client base, and making sure you are legally set up to proceed.

Our team used to use a funny but really important strategy on a common spreadsheet, which is known as the "Eisenhower Matrix Strategy." It is a simple way of categorizing tasks into four different groups: urgent and important, not urgent but important, urgent but not important, and neither urgent nor important. We used to focus on the 'urgent and important' category first and then go ahead, which helped us make the best progress.

I had created a daily routine that helped me to stay organized; each day had specific tasks, like responding to emails, meeting with clients, or reviewing budgets/finances. I used to keep my day step by step, which helped me to stay on track and avoid doing multiple tasks at once.

The temptation to keep working without rest is very strong, especially when you are passionate about your business. In the beginning, I used to work long hours during summer vacations, but I realized that taking breaks and giving myself time to rest is also important. My productivity decreases if I take fewer breaks, although I never pushed myself too much or felt like it was work because I always enjoyed it.

There will always be days when things go well and some days when things fall apart; staying focused during the tough times is what separates successful entrepreneurs from the ones who give up. We faced several such moments where deals were being cancelled at the last moment due to our mistakes, but we stayed focused and reminded ourselves why we had started the business in the first place. Challenges are part of the process and don't define our journey.

KEY TAKEAWAY: EMBRACING THE JOURNEY

As I reflect on the journey so far, the lessons and knowledge I've gained and experienced have affected my personal growth and business both. Entrepreneurship is an unpredictable path. I've learned that persistence is the key. There were times when we felt like we couldn't make it and thought, Is it worth trying more? but the ability to keep going even when things don't go as planned helped me to build something like this. Success doesn't happen overnight, and the key is to always keep learning and pushing forward.

Entrepreneurship is not just about the end goal or making a huge profit; it's about the process, the lessons, the growth, and the knowledge that comes with the journey. I have found that embracing the journey gives more fulfillment than the final outcome; there are always new goals, new challenges, and new opportunities, but as we continue to grow, that's what gives the true experience and happiness.

Chapter 3: The Road to Earning Six Figures

Achieving financial independence as a teenager is not just about earning money, it's about exploring and creating a life where you are in control. Six figures is a milestone that shows a level of success where efforts turn from a hobby to a proper earning business. But what does this mean, and why is it so important?

For many teenagers, financial independence is more than just income. It provides opportunities to explore passion and help develop some practical skills. Stepping into the real world of business and learning the principles of earning, saving, and growing at an early age would help be responsible in the future. By this, we won't be relying on a job or allowance, whether it's travelling, investing in hobbies, or trying new things. We can even invest it in purchasing online courses, hiring a mentor, or getting an opportunity to grow limitlessly.

Six figures is a milestone that many entrepreneurs set as a goal, as it shows significant progress in their journey. When someone reaches this mark, it shows that they have developed a business that works and have the skills needed to improve and expand. Earning six figures helps to handle personal expenses, invest more, and the business is not just a hobby or side hustle; it's a proper business that can support your life sooner or later. Crossing the mark shows that your efforts and strategies are all working and you are on the right path. But once you reach the mark, it's not the end; it's the beginning of more opportunities, like more investments, partnerships, and expansions.

Earning six figures as a teenager is all about developing the right mindset. When you expand and scale up, imagine the freedom of choosing education or career paths without debt or any financial pressure. Support your interests and invest in skills or anything you would like; even if your family would be financially comfortable, it's never wrong to support them more.

Every successful entrepreneurial journey has a powerful vision in the beginning. The vision is not only about the money; it's about what the money would get us. We get the freedom to pursue our own passion, support our family, and have an opportunity to experience the real world. Always create realistic and ambitious goals to be focused. It doesn't only mean hard work but also constantly learning and improving, always reading books, taking courses, and seeking mentorship.

Your mindset plays a very important role in achieving financial independence; you should always focus on growth and value. Always believe that every skill can be learned and you can overcome every challenge; instead of being sad about failure, take it as feedback and improve. You would always have competition and self-doubt but be resilient and focused on your goals. Be consistent, market your product, manage finances, and develop new ideas; keep trying something every day. Financial independence isn't about earning more money; it's about solving a problem. The more value you give to your target audience, the more it grows. Think of the impact you want to leave behind; earning money isn't the end goal; it is the freedom. Always explore interests, take risks, and focus on making something that always works; try automating your business, hiring a team, and dividing your source of income.

You don't need a perfect plan to start; start with basic ideas, give it a time frame, for example, a month, and test it and learn from the process. For example, you are interested in gaming; try coaching, making tutorials, streaming, selling accounts, etc. Another crucial part is to always keep a record of every rupee earned, every client received, and every important lesson learned. Always learn to manage your money and understand customer psychology; network with peers, mentors, and clients. The more you network, the more guidance, support, and opportunities you would receive. Always keep small goals and keep improving; celebrate your first thousand, ten thousand, fifty thousand, and more.

Choose the right niche; it's not about choosing a specific market; choose a place with interest, skills, and market demand. Ask yourself, What am I passionate about? What are my strengths? Think about your hobbies, talents, and knowledge. Identify market trends and demand, evaluate profit potential, and test your ideas. Start small and take feedback; have a clear demand; the niche should be able to grow and not stay constant, having a limited market with lower earning potential. Do not focus on niches that do not interest you, as in the future it would be difficult to stay motivated and improve.

A real-life example would be if you are passionate about video games, try to understand what the players value; many gamers love to buy ready-made accounts, which can get them rare skins, reach a specific rank or level beforehand, and starting with a single game, you can expand to multiple; test by selling accounts you have developed personally or sourcing them through trusted platforms. When you are finding niches, make sure it has long-term potential; don't always look for profit and find something that is long-term and scalable.

A scalable business is the backbone to reaching a bigger goal; it ensures that business can grow and handle increasing demand without increasing costs and a manageable workload. Example: a business that sells a digital product like an ebook or online courses can scale a lot because they can have infinite copies. A service-based business like freelancing is harder to scale unless you have a bigger team, which starts to automate the entire process. Automate repetitive tasks like invoicing, sending pre-made messages, and inventory management. For example, if you are selling gaming accounts, create a platform that would automatically deliver the account as the customer pays so you wouldn't have to be involved. Focus on products or services that would require less effort or expense to make multiple, for example, digital downloads, templates, and guides can be scaled infinitely because they do not have a production cost. Try to use technology to decrease workload instead of depending on other team members; hire freelancers or agencies for tasks like customer service, marketing, and account management.

Define what your product is about and how it sets you apart from your competitors. Make a step-by-step process for delivering your product or service, and make strategies to bring new customers through ads, marketing, or referrals. Create a system to convert leads to proper customers, attract customers through ads, give good offers or information, and simplify the buyer process by making a website or an app. Digital tools are very useful; they can help in organizing, enhancing productivity, and helping focus better to scale your business. In this section, we are going to explore how we can use technology to make smarter decisions, automate tasks, and improve the workflow.

The role of technology is to help small businesses or individuals to compete with bigger organizations; it can help you to access a bigger audience through online platforms, save time by automating repetitive tasks, and analyze data to make better decisions.

These are a few tools that you should consider using:

1. *Project management tools:* There are multiple tools like Trello, Asana, and ClickUp that help to organize tasks, set deadlines, and track progress.
2. *Marketing tools and platforms* like Canva for designing and Buffer or Hootsuite for social media scheduling would help to create and share content online easily.
3. *Customer relationship management software* tools like HubSpot or Zoho CRM help manage customer interactions, track leads, and improve client retention. Try using CRM to maintain a database of customers and track their purchases to send personalized offers.
4. *E-commerce platforms*, such as Shopify, WooCommerce, or Etsy, can be used to set up a simple online store.
5. *Payment gateways*, PayPal, Stripe, or Razorpay also enable foreign customers and have safe online transactions.
6. *Analytics and Insights*, Use tools like Google Analytics and Hotjar to provide insights about customer behavior and website performance, analyze traffic sources, and improve the marketing strategy.
7. *Automation tools*, such as Zapier and Automate.io, are used to connect multiple platforms and automate repetitive tasks, such as email follow-ups after a customer makes a purchase.
8. *Financial management tools*: Personally, I prefer to use websites like QuickBooks, Wave, Xero, or Google Sheets to track income, expenses, and taxes.

Focus on one or two tools that solve your immediate problems; for example, use Canva for marketing and Trello for task management. Always invest in yourself; take online courses or watch tutorials. There are many platforms like YouTube, Udemy, or Skillshare where you can learn how to use these. Choose tools that work together and combine; regularly check the effectiveness of your work from the tools.

For example, you run a business that sells gaming accounts; you can use Canva to make ads and Buffer to schedule them on social media; you can use Zapier to send a welcome email to new customers after they log in or make a purchase; you can use Shopify's dashboard to monitor the revenue and Wave to keep track of expenses and generate monthly reports.

Outline the areas where you need help, find research tools for each area, and pick one that would help you the most or be in your budget; spend proper time setting up each tool to make sure you face no issues later on. As the business grows, you will need advanced tools and strategies; always keep experimenting with new tools and technology.

In your journey, building a personal brand is a necessity; your personal brand is something that makes the customer remember you and not only the company; it helps the customer understand who you are and how you bring value to others. It establishes trust and leads to long-term success. Your personal brand would show your uniqueness and help you stand out from our competitors; instead of being known as a random seller, you could be the first person someone reaches out to to buy something. People are more likely to buy from someone they trust; it turns a one-time customer into lifelong loyal customers.

Reflect on what your brand is trying to show. Example: If your business is about selling gaming accounts, your main aim should be providing easy transactions, affordability, and trust to customers. Always know who you are speaking to, be relatable, and maintain a consistent tone, whether it is professional or casual. Use platforms like Instagram, Facebook, and WhatsApp for brand building; create content that shows your specialty. Share your journey, all the successes, failures, and lessons learned; document the growth of your business from the start.

To turn leads into customers, always exceed the expectations; the main advertisement is to have a satisfied customer sharing their experience. Ask customers to share their experience using your product or service online, and provide discounts or gifts to loyal customers. For example, if you sell gaming accounts, your personal brand should show that you are trustworthy and deliver what you promise to the customers; you should have transparency.

Reaching six figures is a remarkable achievement, but continuing to grow the wealth needs mastering financial literacy, which is to understand how money works, how we manage it, and make decisions that would ensure long-term stability.

Many people who earn a significant amount struggle to hold onto their money because of their spending habits. We need to learn about budgeting, taxes, and investment strategies to ensure the earnings grow rather than decrease. For me, I haven't taken a single profit out as there wasn't anything that I wanted rather than my business to succeed. I used to invest it all again and again. Financial literacy is to keep emergency funds and manage risks properly, expand operations, split income streams, and what helps us to make smarter choices.

KEY PRINCIPLES OF FINANCIAL LITERACY

Keep detailed records of all sources of income, including all businesses and side hustles. I personally use a spreadsheet. Create a budget and categorize expenses into essentials and nonessentials. As the income grows, the liabilities become a lot more complex, including tax liabilities, brackets, etc. Always reinvest in your business; for example, if you are running an editing service, invest in premium software or hire additional editors. Diversify your source of income; try to invest the extra money into stocks or mutual funds. Reinvest a specific percentage of your earnings consistently to scale your business, use profits to enhance marketing efforts or hire more skilled team members, and regularly review your spending and find where costs can be cut out without sacrificing the quality of the work. Don't rely on one source of income; putting all your money into one place can be risky. Spread your investments. Earning six figures is definitely a milestone, but the journey doesn't stop here; make sure you continuously grow and think about scaling your business. Scaling is to increase your business reach and revenue with an increase in the costs. Always work smarter, not harder. Markets evolve, and scaling would help to stay ahead of competitors and make new products or services. Scaling includes automating processes and reducing time spent on repetitive tasks. Try to expand to related niches and find opportunities related to your current business; for example, if you are running a gaming account selling business, you could add gaming accessories like mice, headphones, keyboards, etc., to your stock. Scaling beyond six figures isn't just about being rich; it's about creating a working business for the long term that turns a hobby into a milestone to success.

Reaching the milestone is just more than a financial achievement; it's a journey that is more important than any degree. It shapes our mindset, skills, and how we see life; making our parents proud and celebrating our success is what every teenager wants more than money.
I started with a vision, faced challenges, made tough decisions, and turned ideas into results. Beyond earning money, I feel like I have mastered critical thinking and communication skills, including negotiating and leadership, as I manage a team and handle multiple clients every day. Achieving this milestone has boosted my self-belief a lot too and motivated me for bigger goals; success cannot happen overnight; it requires persistence and dedication. Building strong connections with mentors, partners, and clients is really important.
Your journey should show the power of vision, effort, and resilience; the experience you would gain would continue to help you to make new goals and face bigger challenges, reflect on your achievements, and be ready to improve more.

Chapter 4: Building a Business from Scratch

Starting a business is like building a house; before you put up walls and a roof, you gotta make a strong foundation. These foundation elements are what ensure that your business is capable of growing and staying over time. This chapter would be focusing on products, services, target audience, brand identity, and much more.

Your product or service is the backbone of your business; it is what you are offering. A good product doesn't just exist; it should solve a problem or fulfill someone's need. The more useful and unique a product is, the more valuable it is. If you focus on making your product special, it will create a reason for customers to choose you over competitors.

Ask yourself, what challenges does your product solve? For gaming accounts, it could be the time and effort it takes to level up or getting a rare skin. What makes your product stand out? Is it about the affordability, speed of delivery, or having something rare?

The first step is to identify your audience; it would ensure that you are putting all your energy and efforts into the right place. The more specific we know about your target audience, the easier it is to make a product, marketing, and services. For gaming accounts, your audience might be players from 15-30 who like the specific game. There are many ways to find your target audience: join multiple gaming groups, make a survey, and do direct interviews to understand their needs and preferences. Platforms like WhatsApp and Discord are very famous for this.

Creating a revenue model

A revenue model determines how your business makes money; without clearly understanding it, even the best ideas can fall apart. The main goal is to make such a business that generates income and keeps the buying cost manageable. For example, if your business is about selling gaming accounts, it could be that some accounts could be affordable, and you could keep more premium accounts with exclusive features with higher prices. Think about what the customer would pay for. Is it the product, extra features, or any additional services? Find out how to handle payment transactions; for me, I used to take help from my brother. The most common revenue models are one-time sales, which is to sell a product or service; subscription-based, which can be ongoing per month or per year; and there can also be a free version, which could be providing basic service for free and charging for premium features like Spotify.

Your brand is how customers look at you and what makes them remember you. For a business selling gaming accounts, your brand can be remembered through being trustworthy, fun, and affordable. Every interaction, whether it is social media or an email, reflects your brand's tone, if you are humorous or professional and trustworthy. A strong brand isn't just about having the best logo and designs; it's the experience customers have, how easy your service is to understand or buy, how quickly you respond to inquiries, and more.

CONDUCTING MARKET RESEARCH AND VALIDATION

Launching a business without understanding the market is like sailing a ship without a map; you are just wasting time and resources. Market research is about targeting the right audience, solving the right problems, and being in a place where the demand for your service is present. It includes collecting data, analyzing, and validating ideas before making investments. Let's break it down into simpler and more detailed steps.

Imagine you have come up with a crazy idea for selling sustainable clothing, but you haven't researched if people in your target audience actually value sustainability and are willing to pay for it. Without research, you might spend hours and hours developing a proper website and clothing designs, which would not sell, wasting your own time and resources. Market research helps to learn the audience's preferences, buying behavior, studying your competitors, and validating the demand of your service if the idea has a market that is willing to pay for it.

A successful business solves a specific problem or fulfills a unique need. Ask yourself, what problems does my target audience face, and what are they looking for that they can't find easily? For sustainable clothing, the need could be lack of affordability, eco-friendly options in the current market, awareness of sustainable practices, and more. To identify the need, we can utilize digital tools such as Google Forms to ask potential customers about their habits, for example, how important is sustainability in your purchasing decisions or what challenges do you face when finding eco-friendly clothes? Competitors are not enemies but someone who can give you knowledge; by studying their work, you can find the strengths and weaknesses; you can research brands, look at their work, designs, materials, and pricing.

TESTING YOUR IDEA WITH A MINIMUM VIABLE PRODUCT

A minimum viable product is the simplest version of your product or service. which helps you to find out the demand before fully creating something. It helps you to find out customers without large upfront costs.Customer feedback is really important in refining your product or service. Ask customers what they like, what can be improved, and if they would buy it again. Reach out personally to customers and ask about their opinion; after testing, ask yourself, How many people in my target audience are likely to buy my product? and how much can I sell each product for while maintaining affordability and profitability for both?

Go step by step:

For example, a problem could be local shoppers finding eco-friendly clothing too expensive or unfashionable. Competitor analysis discovered local eco brands charging 10,000 rupees on average. Start by researching to create a better solution, studying your competitors, and improving upon them; try to create a better product for a much cheaper price. Try to design 5 samples and sell them for half the price. Market research and validation are the foundation of a successful business. By understanding your audience, studying competitors, and testing your ideas, you can create a product or service that a customer wants and also stands out in the market.

CREATING A BUSINESS PLAN

A proper business plan is the backbone of any successful venture; it is the roadmap that helps you navigate challenges, attract investors, and stay focused on long-term goals. This section would be focused on creating a realistic business plan focused on your target market and product.

Think of a business plan as a blueprint; without it, you might be building something in the wrong direction. A business plan helps in providing clarity, breaking down your vision into proper steps, helping investors see you have a clear strategy, and acting as a reference to measure progress. An executive summary is a snapshot of your business, which highlights goals, missions, and unique selling points. It contains the name, mission, vision, and the unique selling point. Explain what you are offering and why it matters; be specific and highlight what makes you unique. What problem are you solving? What makes your product unique? Who is your target audience? Market analysis involves deeper understanding of our target audience, industry trends, and competitors. Identify your ideal customer: age, gender, income, lifestyle, and behavior. Highlight key insights about your niche; for example, many studies show that millennials are willing to pay 10-15% more for sustainable products than Gen Z. Find out who is already in the same niche trying out the same as you; for example, competitors like Patagonia focus on premium pricing while Eco trend focuses on affordability. Your business structure determines how your company will legally function, which includes any investors or partners you have thought about. The main things to consider are whether the business would be a sole proprietorship, LLC, or partnership; for example, starting as an LLC ensures personal liability protection and is simple. Ask yourself a question for everything; describe how your operations would evolve as your business grows.

This section is about how to attract customers and generate revenue. Marketing is the bridge between a business and its customer. Make a logo with a color scheme, tone of voice, and a tagline that defines your brand. Decide where you are going to market your products; make a clearer transition for marketing to conversion, for example. You can run Instagram ads and send customers to your website and offer a discount on the first purchase. Always keep financial projections; numbers are very important. Always know your business's earning potential and financial viability. An example of a financial project for the next mponth could be, genwrating a revenue of 50000 by selling 100 units for 500 each. The cost would be 20,000, the marketing budget 5,000, and the profit would be 25,000. By creating a detailed business plan, you set the foundation of your business to grow long-term, attract the right opportunities, and prepare yourself for the challenges ahead.

FINANCIAL PLANNING AND BUDGETING FOR YOUR STARTUP.

Financial planning and budgeting are the backbones of any business. The first step to building a successful business is knowing how much money you would need to start and maintain it. Break down your startup costs into fixed and proper categories. Fixed costs would include expenses like keeping a website online and business licenses, and variable costs could be marketing budgets, materials to make the product, etc. Always keep an emergency fund to cover a fixed amount of a month's expenses in unexpected situations. Imagine starting a subscription box service for stationery; your fixed costs are designing and producing the packaging, and your variable cost depends on how many subscribers you gain. If you estimate these costs, it will help you to price your service accordingly. Always allocate specific amounts for different needs such as marketing, product development, and other expenses. For example, if you have 5000 to start, you might invest 1500 for ads, 1500 for inventory, and 1000 for software or any tools and save the rest. Try utilizing digital budgeting tools such as QuickBooks, Wave, or Google Sheets to track expenses and income. Focus on what gives you the best return on investment; if social media ads give you more sales than influencer partnerships, try allocating more money into ads. Cash flow is the lifeline of any business; it is important to understand and manage the timing of income and expenses. Always know what you are getting paid by customers and when you need to pay suppliers, employees, or any bills. If your business includes invoicing clients, make sure you make proper and legal invoices and set clear payment terms, as late payments could impact your cash flow. For example, a business selling school supplies might have a lot of demand the time before the school year starts and less demand throughout the year. When your savings aren't enough, find ways to get extra funding, start small, and reinvest your earnings into the business; there are many crowdfunding platforms where you can raise money by pitching your business ideas. Many organizxations offr small loans or grants to startiup which focus on sustainbility or community focused intiiatives. Financial planning is not a one-time task; it requires regular monitoring. Dedicate a fixed time each week to review your finances. Once you have a proper cash flow, reinvest profits into areas like product innovation and marketing and expand your team. Mastering these small skills is what makes a strong foundation and gives you control over your business as you grow.

MANAGING RESOURCES EFFECTIVELY

Building a business from scratch requires proper management of time, energy, and human resources and not just financial resources.

Money is often one of the most limited sources for a new business; managing it properly is the difference between failure and success. There are so many steps, such as creating a budget, separating personal and business finance, tracking expenses, having an emergency fund, and so much more.

Time is a finite resource that needs to be managed well, as it can boost productivity and reduce stress. Use digital tools and strategies such as the Eisenhower Matrix to categorize tasks into urgent, important, or delegable. Always break projects into smaller milestones with achievable deadlines; use apps like Clockify to help you track where your time is spent and find areas to reduce and improve. For product-based businesses, inventory management is also very critical to avoid overextending or running out of stock. Technology is like hiring hundreds of people for free; it has automation tools to save time and analytics platforms. It has everything to make the process easier for us, such as automating repetitive tasks like emailing, which saves time and reduces errors. We can utilize tools to track performance, finance, and customer behavior to make better decisions. Sometimes, resources are not physical or tangible, but they are in the form of a connection or relationship. Networking is a very important part of the journey; it helps us gain access to real knowledge, mentorship, and opportunities. A mentor who has been through similar challenges can provide guidance and insights that no website or book can. As a business evolves, the resource needs also do. A startup resource allocation is very different from a properly established business. The more we learn about your industry, customers, and tools, the easier it gets for us to use our resources effectively. We need to invest in growth only when we have the necessary resources to support it; trying to expand too quickly can cause financial and time problems. Effective resource management is all about balancing what we have with what we need to achieve our goals. It can be time, money, skills, or networks; every single resource should be used properly and thoughtfully. The ability to evaluate, allocate, and adapt resources as much as your business grows ensures that you have long-term success and sustainability.

THE ROLE OF LEADERSHIP IN BUILDING A SUCCESSFUL BUSINESS
Leadership is one of the most important factors that determine the success of any business. A great leader should have the vision and know the mission of a business and inspire and guide the team to achieve their goals. This chapter would be focusing on the qualities of effective leadership, the importance of decision-making, and how to have a leadership mindset. Leadership is the ability to be able to influence and guide people towards achieving a goal, which includes setting a direction and motivating others. A leader should have a clear vision and strategy, make good decisions and take responsibility for them, and support and maintain the team. Leaders must have a clear vision of where they want their business to go, ensuring every decision aligns with their company's long-term goals. The business world keeps changing, and a leader's ability to adapt to change is important, being able to make decisions confidently. Taking responsibility for successes and failures and setting an example for the rest of the team. Leadership is not just about individual skills; it's about empowering others to achieve something together. Recognizing and addressing every challenge is part of growing as a leader, managing conflicts, dividing goals into steps, separating tasks, and monitoring progress, staying motivated, and learning from failures. Being a leader means a lot of responsibilities; it is not a one-time achievement; it's a journey of learning and growing; it plays a vital role in the success of any business. It's all about developing the right qualities, being able to make decisions, inspiring your team, and facing challenges. Great leadership is not about controlling people but empowering others to achieve success together.

MAINTAINING WORK-LIFE BALANCE WHILE GROWING YOUR BUSINESS
Entrepreneurship requires long hours and focus, and maintaining a work-life balance is required to have long-term success. As you might have heard this famous quote, "You can't pour from an empty cup." Constant workload can lead to being physically and mentally exhausted, which reduces productivity. A properly rested mind allows you to think creatively and solve problems easily. Maintaining personal relationships provides emotional support. As a business owner, your work habits should influence your team and define when your workday starts and ends. Many entrepreneurs try to do everything themselves, but dividing tasks frees up the time and

makes everything easier. Always take short breaks to recharge, schedule days off to focus on schoolwork, be with family, or relax. Use online tools to reduce unnecessary efforts, such as calendar apps to schedule meetings and task management tools. Try practicing mindfulness and stress management exercises such as starting your day with journaling or meditation and trying physical activities such as any sport or yoga. While putting your full focus on your business, don't' neglect yourself. Always set aside time for yourself to learn new skills, pursuing hobbies or interests. Many entrepreneurs feel that they need to be available 24/7 to be able to catch opportunities; always remind yourself that balance doesn't mean equal time; it means prioritizing what matters more at that moment. "The bad news is time flies; the good news is you're the pilot." - Micheal Altshuler. Remember, maintaining balance is an ongoing process; always know your priorities and adjust your routine. It's not about balancing to be more productive and successful; it's about enjoying the journey of building a successful business.

LESSONS LEARNED: REFLECTING ON STARTING A BUSINESS
Starting a business is like an unpredictable journey; it has its own highs, lows, and lessons that shape our personal growth too. Reflecting on our experiences allows us to understand what worked, what didn't, and how we are as an entrepreneur.
One of the most critical lessons in business is that not even the best idea can succeed without executing it. Perfection is not important at the start; while you wait to perfect your materials, service, or skills, someone else would launch with basic tools and grow from learning. The only thing we need to do is apply. Many successful entrepreneurs agree that failure is not the opposite of success; it is part of the journey to success. Early mistakes teach us resilience; networking, partnerships, and customer relationships are what make or break our business. "Your network is your net worth." - Portal Gale, As a business owner, time is a limited resource; learning how to manage it properly is important. All this can feel overwhelming at times; that's why celebrating small achievements is important. Looking at your progress every day should keep you motivated and remind you why you started this. The most successful entrepreneurs never stop learning; the journey will never be predictable. Taking guidance from those who have walked the same path before you is invaluable. Begin with what you have and build everything from there; learn from mistakes, analyze your failures, and see them as an opportunity to learn. "Success is not final, failure is not fatal: It is the courage to continue that counts." — Winston Churchill. Reflecting on the lessons learned isn't just about looking back; it's about using those lessons to shape our future decisions.
BALANCING PASSION AND PROFIT
When starting a business, one of the biggest dilemmas that entrepreneurs face is how to balance their passion with profitability. Passion gives us the drive to push through tough times and motivates us; it gives us the energy to work long hours and face challenges. No matter how passionate we are, a business without profit would struggle; profits help to reinvest to grow more, but focusing too much on profit affects the quality for the long term. To balance passion and profit, we need to diversify revenue streams, using our passion to create multiple products, such as a wildlife photographer who could sell photos and also give workshops to new photographers. Relying purely on passion leads to overwork; cutting small things to increase profit harms your reputation and integrity. A food company that switches to low-quality ingredients for higher profits would lose their customers as the quality would decrease.

Think about a young entrepreneur passionate about education; he starts by tutoring in person but realizes the limits; to grow his business, he launches an online platform to provide affordable access to education resources, keeps a subscription model to ensure consistent revenue, and keeps engaging directly with students through webinars or live sessions. This aligns with their passion and also allows profitability. Always follow your heart but make smart decisions; focus on both financial growth and personal satisfaction. "Passion is the fuel, but profit is the engine that drives the business forward.".

Chapter 5: The Psychology Of Risk & Reward

UNDERSTANDING RISK IN ENTREPRENEURSHIP

Risk is misunderstood; it is conferred like gambling, a leap of faith without any guarantee of safety. Although for entrepreneurs, it's about embracing and turning something into an opportunity. Every decision, whether it is to launch a startup, try a new market, or make a new product, requires risk. Without risk, there is no reward. Risk in entrepreneurship is facing financial loss, rejection, and many more challenges; they are part of the process. Risk is not something to avoid; it leads to innovation, creativity, and helps to think outside the box.

Take Elon Musk as an example; he risked almost his entire fortune on Tesla, SpaceX, and SolarCity, which led to global success. As he said, "Failure is an option here. If things are not failing, you are not innovating enough".

Risk is what separates dreamers from doers; every idea, like Uber, Airbnb, or Tesla, came with a lot of risk. When Uber launched, people would have never thought they would trust strangers to drive them anywhere; did people think they would let foreigners and strangers enter their homes through Airbnb? These are some ideas that were all developed through taking risks.

Not every risk leads to success; for every company like Apple, there's a BlackBerry; for every Netflix, there's a Blockbuster. Failure happens when risks aren't properly considered. Blockbuster ignored the threat of digital streaming, although Netflix took the risk and won big. Failure is never the end of the road; it's the lesson. As Thomas Edison mentioned while working on the light bulb, "I have not failed. I've just found 10,000 ways that don't work". Every successful entrepreneur sees a failure as a stepping stone and not a stop sign.

It's not about managing risk; it is more about embracing it. Risk forces us to step out of our comfort zone, and that's where the growth happens. As I look back on my journey, I remember many times I regretted my decisions, thinking if I should invest all my savings into an idea and should I quit if something doesn't work, every choice felt difficult; overtime I realized that risk is not something to fear; it's a reminder that we are moving forward.

LESSONS FROM REAL-LIFE ENTREPRENEURS

Let's take some insightful lessons from successful entrepreneurs who have dealt with risks. Sara Blakely, the founder of Spanx, made her billion-dollar company with just $5000. She took a massive risk by quitting her stable job and pursuing an untested idea. She believed in "Don't be afraid to fail. Failure is not the outcome; trying is.

Howard Schultz, the creator of Starbucks, he spent all his life savings on Starbucks; he was turned down by 200 investors, and so many rejections led to one of the most iconic brands in the world. Their stories prove that the bigger the risk, the greater the potential for reward.

In the end, risk is what makes entrepreneurship interesting; it forces you to innovate and keep on moving. It is also a reminder that the journey is as important as the destination; risk teaches us resilience, adaptability, and courage. Some risks pay off, some don't, but every risk teaches us something valuable. As Mark Zuckerberg said, "The biggest risk is not taking any risk. In a world that's changing so quickly, the only strategy that is guaranteed to fail is not taking risks". Entrepreneurship is a game of give and take; we spend hours of hard work and effort hoping for a reward at the end. The reward isn't always money; it's about the experience, the journey, and accomplishment.

Money matters for sure; it is what keeps the business running. It's not just about buying fancy clothes or things. The first time I made a big commission from my business, I invested it back without taking out any profit, and it felt better than everything because I had earned it myself. Satisfaction is a reward that comes from solving a problem of seeing your idea working. Think of non-profit companies like TOMS; for every pair of shoes sold, they donate a pair to someone in need. While their company is profitable, the emotional reward is what they want more than just money. Entrepreneurship forces us to learn and grow in ways no job can ever, pitching investors, brainstorming with a team, and guiding people; the journey itself is a reward. Meeting incredible people, solving problems, facing challenges, and so many stories worth telling.

Why do entrepreneurs chase rewards? Even when the risks are high, it's all about the mindset. It's not just the reward; it's the journey to reach there. Pursuing a goal is as fulfilling as achieving it. The harder the climb, the sweeter the reward; even after falling, we gotta start all over again. Success isn't just about rewards; it's about providing to ourselves what we are capable of. Jeff Bezos once said, "I knew that if I failed, I wouldn't regret that. But I knew the one I might regret is not trying." For Bezos, the reward wasn't just Amazon's success; it was knowing that he took the risk.

Entrepreneurship is a rollercoaster; seeing your idea work, making an impact, or proving to yourself that you can do it is what keeps you going. I remember the time I had reached my goal; it wasn't about the money or the success; it was the joy of knowing I had done something, made something work. We should always dream big, take risks, chase rewards, and enjoy every step of the journey. Because at the end of the day, the greatest success is about the destination; it's the person we become along the way.

The fear of failure is that you would invest time, money, and energy into something that would not work; you think, "What if this doesn't work out?" Failure isn't the opposite of success; it is something that leads to success. Unlike a job where you know how much you are going to earn, entrepreneurship is full of unpredictable moments, which leads us to dream. Many of us think about what others would think if we fail. while we should be the ones laughing that they haven't even made an effort to try. Some people hold themselves back due to fear and stay in their comfort zone rather than taking a risk and failing. Instead of seeing failure in a negative way, take it as feedback; learn something valuable. Someone once told me, If everything feels comfortable, you're not growing."

Risk pushes us to innovate; caution helps us avoid mistakes, and having the right balance between these two is what we need. If every decision you make felt safe, would you ever achieve something extraordinary? "He who is not courageous enough to take risks will accomplish nothing in life." — Muhammad Ali. If you have to make a decision that could make or break your business, for example, signing a contract with an investor, ensure there is nothing that could backfire in the future. Sometimes, the best decision is no decision, as you can't afford to waste money or time. "Don't risk what you have and need for what you don't have and don't need." — Warren Buffett. There is no shame in trying to play it safe when you have such situations. Jeff Bezos, when he launched Amazon, the idea of an online bookstore was risky as technology wasn't used so much during the mid-90s. He didn't put his entire future on day one; he started small, focused on books, and kept expanding to more products as his idea worked. Every time you have to make a big decision, ask yourself if this is a reckless risk or a calculated risk. Am I trying to make safe decisions because I am scared of the outcome or because it's the right choice?

THE ROLE OF CONFIDENCE IN TAKING RISKS

Confidence is something that powers our every step; confidence isn't just about believing in ourselves but building trust in our decisions, instincts, and our ability to recover from a position if things don't go as planned. Confidence helps us to believe in our vision; if we keep overthinking every detail, we miss the opportunity. Would you invest in a founder who doesn't seem sure of their own business? Without confidence, every wrong step feels like a failure; confidence isn't something we are born with; it's something we build with practice, preparation, and perfection. Our confidence grows when we acknowledge our achievements; confidence is about knowing we have done the work. The more prepared we are, the more confidence we feel. Confidence is not about having all the answers and solutions; it means to trust yourself to figure it out along the way. Many think confidence is about never failing, but it's about getting back up after falling. Every mistake teaches us something; confidence comes from knowing failure isn't the end; it's part of the process. "Failure is simply the opportunity to begin again, this time more intelligently." — Henry Ford.

I wasn't always confident; every decision felt like a gamble, and every failure felt like I should not go with this, but I realized confidence isn't just a feeling; it's a skill. It's something that allows us to dream big and take risks, not about being fearless but facing fear, not being perfect but believing in ourselves to be. It's not something we feel; it's something we do.

THE PSYCHOLOGY BEHIND DELAYED GRATIFICATION

Delayed gratification is to resist an immediate reward to get a greater reward later. Many people chase instant wins, but entrepreneurs with a mindset of delayed gratification grind and invest in the process to get a bigger payoff at the end as they believe in patience.

The problem with short-term thinking is that many entrepreneurs fall into this trap and realize they have sacrificed the bigger potential of their idea. Meaningful results take time; it's not about quick wins; it's about building something sustainable and scalable, which requires the discipline to say no to smaller things and focus on the bigger vision.

No successful venture is built overnight; the initial stages of a business are always filled with hard work and low returns. Having a long-term mindset also keeps you calm and persistent, knowing that every small step would lead to a bigger goal. Perseverance is about showing up every day even when the results aren't good; it's about putting in the work, believing in ourselves, and trusting the process. Always adapt, learn, and evolve. Entrepreneurs who follow delayed gratification reinvest their profits into growth rather than taking them out for personal spending. Investors, employees, and customers are more likely to trust an entrepreneur who takes a long-term approach instead of chasing instant results. Visualize your end goal in mind; it will make it easier to stay disciplined. Create a vision board, write down your goals, and remind yourself why you stayed.

"Success usually comes to those who are too busy to be looking for it." — Henry David Thoreau. This quote shows the mindset of delayed gratification, as when we focus on our work and trust the process, success will find us.

RISK TOLERANCE

Risk tolerance is the ability to handle any downsides of a decision; it's not about being fearless; it's about understanding limits and boundaries. "A ship is safe in harbor, but that's not what ships are for." — William G.T. Shedd. In my journey, even small decisions felt overwhelming, but after I was able to achieve a few goals, I began to trust myself, and it made taking risks much easier. Always have a small self-assessment before making a big decision; ask yourself a few questions: What's the worst-case scenario? Can I recover from it? How does the outcome compare to the risk taken? Having a backup plan makes risk-taking more manageable; instead of seeing risks as all or nothing, divide them into smaller steps, like testing a new product with a limited audience rather than launching it. As entrepreneurs grow, so does their comfort zone; risk that once felt like a big step feels like normal. This is a step that shows progress and a reminder that what seems impossible today might feel simple tomorrow. "if you are not a little uncomfortable every day, you're not growing."

Entrepreneurship is all about decision-making; every move comes from a decision and might be made under pressure. Imagine you are in a maze, but someone keeps shifting the walls without telling you. You might think a risky venture would succeed if it reminds you of a past win, or you could hesitate to drop it because of all the time and energy you have invested. There are so many biases that can hold you back, such as trusting your decisions so much that you stop questioning them, following trends because everyone else is, holding onto failing ideas because you have invested a lot of time in them, underestimating risks because success feels easy, and so much more. Overconfidence is not always bad; it can lead you to make bold steps that no one else does. "The key to success is not being right all the time but being willing to challenge yourself when you're strong." If you can master your mind, you can master your business. Entrepreneurs are born as risk-takers; we develop our skills through experience and learning. Many people who have learned to see failure as a step and not the end understand that every risk can be a threat or an opportunity. As you move forward in your journey, take time to reflect on the risks, the lessons, and the rewards you have earned along the way. Reflection isn't just to look back; it's about finding meaning and using your past knowledge to improve. When I started, I made a lot of mistakes when the risks seemed too high and the rewards didn't feel worth the risk. I pushed through and always found myself closer to my thoughts. Entrepreneurship is not easy math but has the most rewarding journey as one of the best businessmen. Richard Branson said, "The best way of learning about anything is by doing."

Take that risk, dream big; even if you fail, keep going. The greatest rewards lie on the other side of the scariest risk.

Chapter 6: Networking and Intersection of Technology

Starting a business decades ago used to be a crazy task; we needed a lot of money to rent or buy space, hire employees, and invest in inventory and machines. Advertising was slow and expensive, relying on things like billboards, newspapers, and radio. Communication with customers took time and effort. But when we look at it today, technology has transformed the way businesses are created and grow. It speeds us up and simplifies every process to turn an idea into a successful business. It reduces cost, saves time, connects us everywhere, and whatnot.

Technology has made starting a business much easier; we don't need years of experience or a lot of money. We can create extraordinary things with just a device and wifi; for example, a platform like Shopify helps people create online stories in just hours without needing much technical knowledge. Innovation starts by solving a problem; technology helps us give the tools to identify and fix problems quickly. For example, AI can be used to analyze big data and help businesses understand their data. Previously, scaling up meant opening in more places, increasing staff, and making more things, but digital tools make scaling so much easier.

Netflix is one of the best examples of how technology leads to innovation. It started as a DVD rental service where customers ordered DVDs online and Netflix mailed them. But as technology advanced, Netflix turned into a streaming platform; it also uses data analytics and AI to understand what people want to watch, which has led it to dominate the entertainment industry.

Technology enables us to work from anywhere; we can access any tools online, such as Canva, Wix, Slack, and so many more. For me, I used Trello; it is a free task management app that is used to organize projects, which helped me to break down bigger tasks easily. "Innovation distinguishes between a leader and a follower"—Steve Jobs. This quote reminds us that using technology to innovate is about leading the way and finding new solutions. We can turn any idea into reality with the right tools and mindset.

Digital transformation is something we hear all the time; it's about the integration of technology to improve how businesses operate and give value to customers. It's not about replacing manual processes; it's about rethinking and reshaping the way industries work by solving problems in smarter ways, being faster, and being more efficient. A few decades ago, shopping was just to visit a store and wait in checkout lines, but today we can buy almost anything sitting in our homes. Platforms like Amazon and Flipkart have revolutionized retail by offering customers such a big variety of products at good prices with just a few clicks of a button. Example: during the COVID-19 pandemic, small businesses had to learn about digital transformation to survive; many set up online stores and used Instagram shopping and WhatsApp business to sell their products.

Traditional education relied heavily on classrooms, but technology made it more flexible, interactive, and accessible. There are so many platforms, such as Coursera and Khan Academy, which make it possible for students to learn from anywhere. For healthcare, technology apps like Practo allow patients to book appointments with doctors online, wearable devices such as Fitbit monitor to measure your health in real time, and hospitals have also started using AI-powered diagnostic tools to detect diseases with higher accuracy. Before, cash and checks were the only ways to pay, but there are digital wallets such as Paytm, Google Pay, and many more to make transactions quick and easy.

The main benefits of digital transformation are that businesses save time and money by automating repetitive tasks, it creates a better customer experience, and it has a global reach. But the main challenge is that not everyone is good with technology, and as the businesses are online, there is a lot of risk of data breaches. When I think about how technology has transformed industries, as a student, I have used apps like Paytm for transactions, Coursera for courses and learning new skills, and Netflix for entertainment, all just sitting at my time. It would have been a hassle to access all this without digital transformation. "The best way to predict the future is to create it." — Peter Drucker, digital transformation is something that is going to help us thrive in today's world.

EMERGING TECHNOLOGIES

Emerging technologies are transforming how businesses operate; it makes them faster, smarter, and more efficient. It's not optional; it's essential for being competitive and innovating in today's world. For example, artificial intelligence helps to analyze big amounts of data quickly, automate tasks like customer support through chatbots, and optimize strategies. Technologies like the Internet of Things (IoT) are also transforming industries by connecting devices to share real-time data and monitor operations and improving efficiency. Emerging technologies are not limited to specific industries; augmented reality and virtual reality are reshaping customer experience in sectors like real estate, education, and retail. Cloud computing has simplified business operations by allowing entrepreneurs to store and access data without expensive hardware investments, which makes it the best tool for startups. Such advancements have led to so many benefits, including cost savings, faster innovation, and enhanced customer experience. To conclude, emerging technologies are more than just tools; they are essential for innovation and growth, and by using such tools, we can optimize our businesses, connect with the global market, and stay ahead of our competitors.

There are a lot of challenges, such as cybersecurity. Imagine spending years building your customer base and gathering valuable data, and a hacker gains access to the customer data, and your company's reputation is on the line. In 2017, Equifax, one of the largest credit reporting agencies in the US, suffered a breach that exposed personal data of 147 million people, which led to a lot of financial costs and consumer distrust. The idea of securing their business's data can be difficult; investing in strong cybersecurity practices like using encryption, firewalls, and good passwords can make a difference. Even though many technologies offer great services, the cost can be too much, especially for startups, using advanced software subscriptions and hardware upgrades. Prioritize spending on technologies that help you scale and boost productivity; a tool that automates tasks and improves communication would pay for itself by saving time and focusing on growth. Although every problem can be solved, which means that a business can become stronger and more capable of competing in the market, never let fear of change hold you back. "The only constant in life is change," and embracing technology is the way.

HOW ENTREPRENEURS CAN HARNESS EMERGING TECH

The digital world is evolving at a really fast pace, with new technologies coming every day that would reshape industries and bring new opportunities. For entrepreneurs, staying ahead and adapting to things beforehand is an advantage and essential for growth.

When people hear blockchain, they think of things like bitcoin or cryptocurrencies, although blockchain technology is more than that and a way to transact digital currencies in a secure, transparent, and tamper-proof way. Which means that businesses can use blockchains to create more trustworthy systems for tracking and verifying transactions. Blockchain allows businesses to track products from source to consumer with proper accuracy, which reduces fraud. For example, IBM's Food Trust Network uses blockchain to track the journey of food from farm to table; consumers can also trace their food back to its origin with transparency and safety.

Artificial intelligence is not just a futuristic concept anymore; it's transforming how businesses operate. Chatbots, recommendation engines, automating tasks, enhancing customer service, decision-making, and whatnot. We can utilize AI to improve efficiency and even for analyzing data. AI is particularly being used a lot for customer service, such as chatbots, which provide 24/7 support to customers and solve problems without involving real humans, which allows businesses to give immediate services without any extra efforts or costs. For example, Netflix's recommendation engine uses AI to analyze user behavior and suggest shows or movies based on their previous watching habits.

Augmented reality is also a new technology that provides businesses with a unique way to engage customers and differentiate themselves in the market. It allows customers to interact with products in any news and create a new experience. AR can revolutionize the online shopping experience as customers can try on clothes and visualize furniture and objects in their homes without purchasing anything. The IKEA Place app uses AR to let users visualize how different things would look in their homes, which makes it more convenient and easy to make their decisions. We can take advantage of technology and learn about it by attending events, courses, webinars, and resources available and apply it to our business. By staying open to new ideas, we can unlock new ways to improve our business, so start exploring these technologies and have long-term success. "I helped a man climb a mountain and found that I too had reached the top.".

Chapter 7: Through the Lens of Growth: My Journey Unraveled

Starting a business as a teenager was not just an experiment; it was a complete transformation in how I viewed life, work, and the world around me. Even though there might be self-doubt and hesitation, those were the lessons that shaped who I really became today. Success isn't built on luck; it's carved out of decisions, failures, focus, hard work, and creativity.

As I moved forward, I started to realize something powerful: success isn't a destination; it's not about the money you make or the milestones we hit; it's about who we became in the process. At the end I realize these lessons weren't just about building my business; they were about building myself, learning to trust myself, adapting to challenges, and valuing the relationships I have. This journey wasn't a test of my skills; it was a reflection of my ability to be able to rise, learn, and thrive, and according to me, that is what defines success. I can say that this journey taught me how to rise, not just in business but in life. *"Success isn't the key to happiness. "You don't have to be great to start, but you have to start to be great."* — Zig Ziglar

LESSONS LEARNED ALONG THE WAY

"Success is not final, failure is not fatal; it is the courage to continue that counts." — *Winston Churchill*

One of the biggest lessons I learned is that failure doesn't define you; it's how you respond to it that shapes who you become. In the start, failure felt like a heavy weight pressing me down; the fear of making a mistake held me back. I came to see that those mistakes weren't things to be ashamed of but stepping stones. I took every failure as feedback; it wasn't the end; it was an opportunity to build something big.

This journey taught me that "perfection is an illusion" and the pursuit of it often wastes time. When we build something from scratch, we don't have the time for everything to line up perfectly. I realized that this business wouldn't wait for me to get comfortable. I had to get used to being uncomfortable with learning as I moved on.

It felt like I was learning new things every single day; adaptability was an important skill, and there were no guides or clear roadmaps, so I was creating my own way using lessons learned through trying. Distractions are endless; I always reminded myself that building something worthwhile takes time and a lot of commitment. It's not about doing everything at once; it's about doing what matters most and doing it well. *"Success is the sum of small efforts, repeated day in and day out."* — *Robert Collier.*

One of the main things in this journey was patience; success isn't instant; it's showing up every day and trusting yourself and your efforts that they would be worth the time. One of the most powerful lessons I have learned is that the journey is more important than the destination; the real growth happens in the process. The days when everything feels like it's falling apart, those are the moments that forge your character. What you gain along the way—resilience, persistence, and believing in your ability to figure things out—are the real treasures of the journey.

FAILURES THAT FUELED GROWTH

"Failure is simply the opportunity to begin again, this time more intelligently." — *Henry Ford*

Failure wasn't just a part of the journey; it was the force behind my growth. I knew I would face failures, but I wasn't prepared for how deep the lessons from failure would be. But I realized that *"Failure isn't the opposite of success; it's part of it."* Every setback was a lesson I didn't know I needed. It's okay to fail fast, as the faster we fail, the quicker we learn. I always took a step back and tried to find what went wrong to improve the next time, which taught me to adapt and be more decisive. I learned how to handle pressure and how to prepare better for the next opportunity. Success isn't about avoiding failure; it's about how you rise from it; it's about being able to keep moving forward. I would have considered failures as losses at the start, but now I see them as stepping stones. With each failure, I learned to trust my gut more; I learned to own my decisions. The more I failed, the more I grew my confidence and self-reliance. If there's one thing I learned from all this, *"it's that failure doesn't end your journey; it redefines it"*.

THE PERSONAL GROWTH BEHIND THE BUSINESS

"The only limit to our realization of tomorrow is our doubts of today." — Franklin D. Roosevelt
Starting a business was never just about building something crazy; it was a journey of personal transformation. My focus was on goals like being profitable and getting recognition. But over time, I started to realize something more meaningful: the real success wasn't in the business I was building; it was in the person I was becoming.

Entrepreneurship hasn't just taught me how to run a business; it taught me how to face life's challenges. There were days I felt like I was carrying the weight of the world on my shoulders; each challenge was an opportunity to prove to myself that I could handle more than I thought. The real lesson was that it wasn't about perfection; it was about perseverance. I was able to maintain a balance; I realized that success wasn't about sacrificing everything for the business but rather learning how to balance both personal and professional life. The more I understood myself, the more I was able to leverage that knowledge to make better decisions for the business and my life. *"The greatest glory in living lies not in never falling, but in rising every time we fall." — Nelson Mandela*

As I look back now, I can see how far I've come, not just in the business but as a person. It's not just about making money; it's about becoming a stronger and more capable version of yourself.

RELATIONSHIPS AND CONNECTIONS

"Success is never a solo journey. It's built on the bridges we create, the bonds we nurture, and the connections that inspire us to reach greater heights."
Starting a business was also about reshaping the relationships and connections that surround me. When I started this journey, I had no idea how a relationship with others would influence my growth. At the start, I was spending too much time and energy on work, and I started to feel like I was keeping my personal relationships away by spending less time with friends and family. I began to notice the distance I was unintentionally making between myself and the people who cared about me. A close friend once asked me, "Do you even have time for yourself anymore?" That made me realize how addicted and focused I got into the work that I was breaking the connections in my personal life. Balancing work and personal life wasn't easy; what I learned was that relationships thrive not on grand gestures but on small and consistent acts of presence and care.

Entrepreneurship taught me that while the journey is deeply personal, the bonds we nurture, the support we give and take, and the people we surround ourselves with are like the threads that weave our stories into something greater than ourselves.

FACING PERSONAL SACRIFICES

Success, no matter how fulfilling it is, always has a cost. When I decided to start my journey, I knew there would be sacrifices, but I underestimated just how much it would be. While others might have been living carefree lives, I was spending a lot of time, energy, and focus.

The main sacrifice was time; it wasn't about giving up free time or spending less time on social media; it was my entire schedule. It came to a point where I felt like I had no schedule at all; sometimes I was awake till late at night, not because I had to complete something, but because I enjoyed it too. But those were moments with people I cared about that I could never get back. I didn't regret working hard, but I would be lying if I said it didn't hurt to feel disconnected at times. *"Every yes to your dreams is a no to something else, and every no carries a weight."* Financially, the sacrifices were just as real; all of my earnings—100% of it—went back into the business. I was focusing on building something long term; it's hard to watch experience the 'now' while I bet everything on a 'someday.' There were moments of overwhelming doubt where I questioned if the sacrifices were worth the reward. But over time, I learned that sacrifices aren't about giving things up; it's about trading them for something you believe is worth more.

"The bridges we burn for our dreams don't leave us stranded; they force us to move forward." What I have also realized is that sacrifices aren't just about loss; they're about trust. Trust in yourself, your vision, and the journey ahead. Sacrificing the instant award for the long term, and in all the process, growing in ways we can never expect.

Surely I have missed out on experiences and moments, but what I have gained was more valuable: *"Sacrifices don't break you; they shape you."* Looking back, I know the sacrifices I made were important; each one taught me a valuable lesson: time is precious, relationships require balance, and purpose is what makes the trades worth it. The person I've become, resilient, focused, and confident, wouldn't exist without those choices.

HOW I DEFINE SUCCESS NOW

Success for the longest time is a concept that lived all about numbers: How much money can I earn? How many deals can I close? How fast can I grow my business?. But as I moved deeper into my journey, I started to realize that success isn't something you chase; it's something you redefine.

In the beginning, I was so focused on results; every milestone was like a validation that I was on the right path, but as time went on, those small victories were important but started to feel like nothing. They were a bit exciting, but they didn't have the depth I expected.

"Success isn't about what you achieve. It's about what you become in the process."

The more I worked, the clearer everything became, but I didn't feel enough to sustain. They felt like hollow unless they had a deeper meaning to it. I began asking myself questions: Was I proud of the way I achieved these wins? Was I making an impact beyond the balance sheet? Success now feels different; it's quieter and personal. It's no longer about chasing a specific destination; it's about being present in the journey, finding meaning in the work I do, the relationships I have, and the lessons I learn along the way. One of the most important lessons I learned was that success is not universal; it's deeply personal. The perspective didn't develop easily; there were moments of comparison, looking at others who seemed to achieve more, faster, with less effort, but I realized that comparing your journey to someone else's is the fastest way to rob yourself of joy. "Your success doesn't need to look like anyone else's." It just needs to feel right for you.

For me, success is now about balance; it's about having the time and space to pursue my passions without losing the people who care for me and missing out on teenage life. It's about resilience, the ability to adapt and grow no matter the challenges. I've also learned that success is measured not just by the moments but in how we handle moments of failure: "True success isn't about reaching the top; it's about who you've become by the time you get there." It's not about a single moment or milestone; it's about living a life that aligns with my values, pursuing the goals that challenge me, and appreciating the lessons that come along the way. It's about knowing and understanding that even when the world feels uncertain, I am able to move forward.

LOOKING BACK, LOOKING FORWARD

As I reflect on this journey, one thing is very clear: nothing about this experience was an accident. Every night, every challenge, every setback was a step forward even if it didn't feel like that at the time. We only see the pattern when we look back, and looking back, I see a version of myself who didn't know much they were capable of. I wasn't born with a proper business brain or crazy confidence; I was someone who was able to push forward, as giving up just didn't feel like an option.

"You don't find strength by avoiding the fire; you find it by walking through it."

The lessons I've learned go far beyond just business; I've learned to trust myself and my instincts, and I've learned that failing isn't the opposite of succeeding but a part of it. I've learned that resilience is less about being unshaken and more about standing back up, no matter how many times you fall.

When I think about the person I was when I began, I feel a quiet and steady pride, not because I could achieve something, but because I stayed in the fight. I learned how to adapt, how to be patient, and most importantly, how to believe in myself. The self-belief wasn't there at the start; it was earned through the process.

Looking forward, the road feels like like unchafrterd terriotiy which doesn't scare me anymore Ike it used to. I know now that I don't need all the answers, a perfect map, or a proper guide. What I need is the courage to take the next step, the humility to keep learning, and the resilience to keep showing up.

"The past doesn't define you, but it prepares you for what comes next."

This journey, while life-changing, is just a foundation; it's not the final chapter of my story; it's the start. Everything I've learned so far, from the lessons in failure to the moments of triumph, has just shaped me for the next stage. The tools I've gathered, the strength I've built, and the vision I have sharpened are just the beginning of something far greater.

Looking ahead, I don't see an easy path. I know there are going to be more challenges testing me just like the ones before, but I also see endless opportunities, and that's what excites me most, the possibilities I haven't yet imagined.

"Success isn't reaching the top; it's learning how to climb."

I don't want to replicate the past; I want to grow from it. The lessons I've learned will guide me, but they won't hold me back. I'm not the same person I was when I started this journey, and I won't be the same person when I take the next step. Growth isn't about staying the same; it's about evolving, adapting, and striving for more.

There's freedom in knowing that the possibilities are endless, that I can redefine success with every new chapter.

Looking back, I am thankful for every struggle, I'm thankful for every failure, and I'm thankful for the wins that reminded me why I started. Most of all, I am thankful for the chance to grow into the person I've become; looking forward, I know the best is yet to come.

This journey didn't just teach me how to build a business; it taught me how to build myself, and that, I believe, is the most valuable success of all.

A PERSONAL THANK YOU TO MYSELF

In this crazy whirlwind of ambition, failures, and triumphs, I have also paused to thank the mentors who guided me, the friends who encouraged me, and the family who stood by my side. But now, as I reflect on everything I've been through, I realize there is someone else who deserves gratitude: myself.

Yes, me, the version of myself that dared to dream when the world whispered doubts, the version that fought through the anxiety of, "What if this is just a waste of time? the one who didn't stop when things got hard. Today, I recognize that my greatest ally was always the one staring back at me in the mirror.

"The hardest battles are the ones you fight with yourself, but those are the victories that truly count."

To the teenager who started this journey without any guarantees, thank you for trusting the process. I know the hesitation you felt, the fear of what others might think, yet you continued to be uncertain and thought, "Why not me? That decision changed everything.

To the version of me who faced failure head on, thank you for refusing to let it define you. I remember those moments, the deals that fell apart, the mistakes that cost more than they should have, and many more setbacks. You didn't break; you adapted, and in the adaptation, you became someone stronger, sharper, and more determined.

"Failure wasn't a setback—it was the fire that forged me into something unbreakable."

To the version of me who kept showing up when no one was watching, thank you for your discipline; success isn't about talent or luck; it's about consistency; to the version of me who celebrated small victories and found joy in the process. Who taught me that success isn't about the milestones; it's about appreciating the progress, the lessons learned, and the moments.

"Success isn't the trophy at the finish line—it's the resilience you build while running the race."

Writing this chapter feels surreal; it's not just the end of a book; it's the end of a chapter in my life that's been nothing short of transformative, and when I look back, I can see not just a business that grew but a person alongside it. And if there's one thing I learned, it's: *"The greatest reward of success isn't what you achieve—it's who you become in the process."*

The dreamer, the doer, the survivor, the one who weathered storms, embraced chaos, and turned failure into momentum; this journey wasn't just about building a business; it was about proving to myself that I could. That I was capable. That I was enough.

Always remember, you are your own foundation. The gratitude you owe yourself is immeasurable. And when you take a moment to thank yourself for your courage, resilience, and growth, you will realize that the person you've become is your greatest success of all.

"The greatest pleasure in life is doing what people say you cannot do." - Walter Bagehot